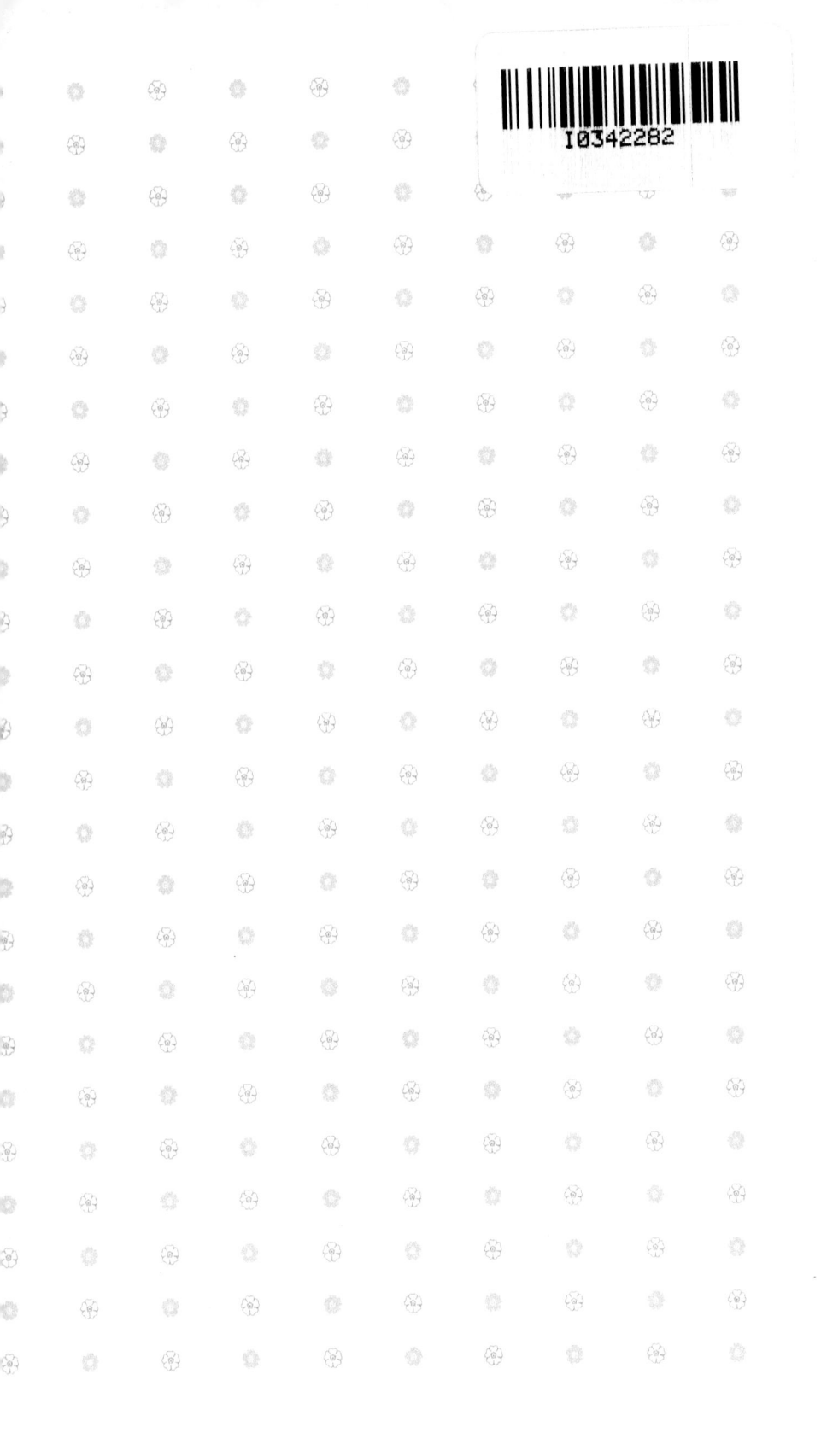

## in case of emergency press

We are proud to acknowledge the Traditional Owners of country throughout Australia and to recognise their continuing connection to land, waters, and culture. We pay our respects to their Elders.

We support recognition, reconciliation, and reparation.

# Two Tongue World

*The Diaspora Dialogues*

## Maria Koukouvas

**in case of emergency press**
*https://icoe.com.au*
Travancore, Victoria
Australia

Published by in case of emergency press 2023

Copyright © Maria Koukouvas 2023
All rights reserved. Without limiting the rights under copyright reserved above, no part of this publication may be reproduced, stored in or introduced into a database and retrieval system or transmitted in any form or any means (electronic, mechanical, photocopying, recording or otherwise) without the prior written permission of both the owner of copyright and the above publishers.

ISBN: 978-0-6458496-1-5

*Cover painting*: Desma Kastanos

# Acknowledgements

Arachne's Thread—*The Victorian Writer*
Bucket of Fish—*The Saltbush Review*
Dogolalia—*The Victorian Writer*
Chicken Bones—*Cordite Poetry Review*
Fire—*Canberra Times Panorama Literary Supplement*
Goat Bell Sonata—*Echidna Tracks Blog*
Grace—*InDaily Newspaper*
Greece-A Quintet—*Beyond the Bend, Friendly Street Poets Anthology 47*
Pig Foot—*SCUM Magazine*
Sonnet to Mother's Eyes, Aegean Dreaming, Magnified, Father Refound, Eyes Like Black Plates, The Unvisited Graves of Priests—*Friendly Street New Poets 19*
The Body Mother Made Me—*Grieve Anthology 2017, Hunter Valley Writer's Centre, Friendly Street New Poets 19, InDaily Newspaper*
The Orphaning—*Kaleidoscope, Friendly Street Poets Anthology 44*
Woman is the Cow of the World—*Newcastle Poetry Prize Anthology 2020*

*All poems originally published under the name Maria Vouis*

# Dedication

For my mother Kalliope Epitropoulos and father Antionios Koukouvas. For their courage to leave their home country, carrying two infants, trunks and suitcases, without language or family support, to make a life in South Australia during the migrations of the 1960s.

To all migrants who gave their skills and youth to build Australia's nationhood.

# Table of Contents

| | |
|---|---:|
| **The Orphaning (i)** | **1** |
|    Fire | 3 |
|    Sonnet to Mother's Eyes | 4 |
|    The Orphaning | 5 |
|    My Father's Last Cigarette | 7 |
|    The Zeibekikos | 8 |
| **Mother Tongue** | **11** |
|    Pig Foot | 13 |
|    Magnified | 15 |
|    The Rule of the Gap | 16 |
|    My Mother at the Well | 18 |
| **Steeling My Childhood** | **19** |
|    Tin-Shed Church | 21 |
|    Bucket of Fish | 23 |
|    Red Piano Accordion | 24 |
|    Old Spice | 26 |
|    Grace | 27 |
| **Harlot Times Two** | **29** |
|    Scream | 31 |
|    Shadow Stain | 33 |
|    Curse of Beauty | 35 |
|    Cinderella's Zorba | 36 |
|    Bravo! | 39 |
| **The Orphaning (ii)** | **41** |
|    The Body Mother Made Me | 43 |
|    Aegean Dreaming | 44 |
|    The Angiogram | 46 |
|    Cake of the Dead | 49 |
|    Chicken Bones | 50 |
|    The Unvisited Graves of Priests | 52 |
|    Wick | 53 |

| | |
|---|---:|
| **Hymn of Belonging** | **55** |
|     Earth My Body | 57 |
|     Greece | 59 |
|     Whose Are You | 60 |
|     Arachne's Thread | 62 |
|     Dogolalia | 64 |
|     Little White House | 65 |
| **Two Tongue Love** | **69** |
|     Father Refound | 71 |
|     Eyes like Black Plates | 72 |
|     Τρυφερός | 73 |
|     Fruit of Exile | 74 |
|     Rachmaninov's Vespers | 76 |
| **Tongue Song for Women** | **79** |
|     Washing | 81 |
|     Woman is the Cow of the World | 82 |
|     The Offering | 84 |
|     Coffee Cup | 86 |
|     Thirteen Ways of Looking at a Fig | 87 |
|     Three Dips | 89 |
|     Through the Mouth | 91 |
| **Epilogue** | **93** |
|     Babel Box | 95 |
|     Space and Wind | 98 |
| **Author's Notes** | **103** |
| **About the Author** | **105** |

# Two Tongue World

*The Diaspora Dialogues*

**Maria Koukouvas**

"...a migrant has lost a home rather than a country and he taps in vain at the window of his past."

A Foreign Wife, Gillian Bouras.

# The Orphaning (i)

# Fire

My father's forearms are on fire,
he holds them forth
above the heater,
a blazing forked prayer
to the God of English.

Outstretched arms in
supplication to reveal to him
the difference between
kerosene and petrol.

My four-year-old eyes
mirror the crawl of flame and fear.
I hear his invocation in panicked Greek,
a plea in lyric lalia.

To the tongues of ancient muses
he cries to unravel the mystery
of this alien patois, in this new land,
to speak it fast enough to survive.

# Sonnet to Mother's Eyes

Sometimes when I get home, I think Mother
is still alive, still there waiting for me,
still have things to tell her I discover,
I trill with things to spill, what could they be?
How well I sang tonight, which dress I wore,
how they loved that chiming voice she gave me.
She wanted to know this and so much more;
she listened gimlet-eyed with pride and glee.
This mute, patient mother for whom I spoke,
placed me as passport to the two-tongue world,
I was her eyes, ears, mouth: my childhood work
to feed her migrant's mind all it could hold.
Dear Mother, my burden, my true witness,
shelter from my father's scorn and bleakness.

# The Orphaning

The orphaning happens
even while your family lives.
Winged through an ocean of mumming cloud,
you are suddenly doubled in tongue
and halved by hearth,
spat through the birth canal
of thundering engines and turbulence,
wailing in words unknown to your host.

Your shrunken family
camps in a glassed-in veranda
whose blue wall papers your diaspora dreams,
your home is a Lego of luggage,
labyrinth trunks and suitcases
you stumble your first steps between.

Then you learn to scribble your childhood days
onto a red-dirt page with salt-bush punctuation,
scribing a language that splits your mind
in a school that spruiks French, German, English,
but no mother tongue, and you live
in your parents' question of why you came.

Your mother mouths her pain
in gibberish to the Australian doctor
and your 10-year-old self learns to be
a small social worker, nurse, a personal shopper,
translator of adult mysteries.

Soon, your parents age then die,
their blanked brains shut a dark door

on a library of stories and snapshots
of you and your ilk, smiling
in the milk-light of your island home.

They are buried in this alien earth
and your infant self is buried with them
in an unmarked orphan's grave.

# My Father's Last Cigarette

I am swinging in the sun
soaking my two-year-old skin,
this sun I will later crave to swallow
in the smelting ground slum
of Whyalla and BHP,
red powder earth, salt bush,
council hutches for migrant labourers
and the afterthought of their families.

The luminous white courtyard
of my first and only home,
built by grandfather's hands,
now a crumble of bulldozers,
a phallus of flats rises in its place.

My father's last Greek cigarette
burns into the arc of ashes
our lives will become,
the curve of his foreign grave.
He does not know this.

# The Zeibekikos

## *The Music is a Beast*

On a stamp-sized stage I'm wedged between bouzouki and oud,
my song strained through drones from antique wood,

then nailed to steely descants that slice air, trace the *'drómous'*[1],
those exiling roads from Smyrna to Athens

my ancestors trod, dropping like beaten olives,
their blood and oil eaten by the passing Turkish earth.

My soprano sounds too pretty for Rembetica,
these soiled works of Ataturk's eviction,

too coy for conviction and exodus, for those trails
that knit a knot of drugs, disease and despair

poured into the port of Piraeus, slums where
my family claimed home. There and here this music

is a homeless beast, bellows minor keys and modes,
drummed to delirium, its syncopated spine spins stories

the hypnotic hiccup of the Zeibekikos beat,
its steps a stutter of naked pain.

The ageless beast stamps, ringed by its worshippers,
a chain of hand-clasp links, feet crossing, uncrossing,

old men bow white heads, arms like migrating cranes,
hop, jump and twirl on their refugee soles,

---

[1] *'drómous'*, is the Greek word for both roads and musical keys.

white handkerchiefs flutter, a flag of freedom,
*never surrender, never surrender,*

womens' arms yoke across each other's breasts,
like the women of Souli held infants in their dance to death,

shuffling from the Ottoman's chains,
this rhythm sobs, throbs then refrains.

At midnight, I deliver my swansong—*Tzivaeri*,
the Greek *Danny Boy*, the dirge of diaspora,

my notes glissando over the wilderness
of pulsing crowd, sweat and speed,

the microphone vacuums my voice,
splinters it through the horseshoe of dancers,

my legato marries the primal moan, a few random notes
rebound in tones I cannot recognise as my own.

Its life unleashed the beast pumps through the small hours,
on without relent until each bracket is spent

and I am pinned between bouzouki and oud,
on a stamp-sized stage, helpless and want to cry.

# Mother Tongue

# Pig Foot

>        *Peeg foot, peeg foot.*
My mother vaults the words over
the Woolie's meat counter,
shouting it louder and louder
just as she called family names across
the flat white roofs of her village.

No friendly echo here,
just a sneer from
the Anglo girl guarding
lamb chops, Epping sausages and
a mesmerising log of mettwurst.

My five-year-old eyes
scale the skyscraper of curved glass,
roll with the sweep
of my mother's semaphore,
reel back to the rufous cheeks
of the Viking-blonde meat-maiden,
queen of this carnal Valhalla,
whose satellite-dish ears
are too rusted to receive
this New Australian's signal.
>        *Peeg fooot, peeg fooot, yooo heeve peeg foot?*

Her sounds thicken and stew,
stretched English vowels
and lisped consonants
splatter from her lips.
>        *Peeg fooot, peeg foot.*
>        she mimes a charade

of the pig's trotter my father needs
to make the pork in aspic dish
he continued to cook
until his last days.

Her query hangs frantic and unrequited
in the supermarket's smelly air
and we go without that magic bowl
with its little sea of soupy jelly,
bay leaf, peppercorn and pork, conjured
from the throw-away parts of the pig.

They, the poor,
used *all* the animal,
slaughtered in the names of their saints
and only ever on Holy feasts.

Between beasts,
it was just beans and bread.

# Magnified

Liquid with love and loss, your mother's eyes
loom as large at street's end as at your gate.
Memory, a sea of myth magnifies,
but her eyes still hold yours and you are late.
Through the morning's door, child-step like a thief
shoulder-checking, yes, her vigil remains.
Her brown eyes track you with their lode of grief,
stalk and soak you like a mammary stain.
All buzzing-fly, hot, sweating school-day long,
back and forth, your thoughts, her speechless sendings,
Greek threads, in your schoolbag knotted strong,
her waiting for every school-day's ending
to search the maze of your new English tongue;
you, losing her language while still so young.

# The Rule of the Gap

The sounds that wagged my infant tongue
are not the ones that move it now.
When bookless and chattering
I went to school, I learned the rule of the gap:
      the gap in time, the silence, the inhale hiss and then:
         *K-k-k-k-k-k-kou-kou-k-k-k-k-kou-vas?*
The teacher's tongue stuttered,
day in, day out, the machine-gun roll call
of my butchered name,
the whole shrapnel, school year long.

My brown eyes flooded
and swam the dirty, carpet-tile sea
that parted me from a whitewash of children
on their island in the corner,
swirling, worshipping a tall woman,
pink lipstick spilling a cadence of code,
body tall as the tower of Babel.

My four-year-old mouth mimed a question
muffled through the maelstrom
of pale-skinned, blonde kids
screeching like the demented, dancing birds
in the scented eucalyptus trees.

I entered my first day's classroom speaking
and left it at day's end, speechless,
but my child-brain bloomed strange fruit
hung in this new tree of knowledge:
      I was a 'kou-kou',
        a swarthy-skinned cuckoo,

not a pink and white fairy-bread
sprinkle sandwich galah like them;
not a happy, little Vegemite,
but a salami-lunch-toting
nest-stealing, cuckoo 'wog'.

Where is my mum? Πού είναι η μαμά μου; *Poú eínai i mamá mou?*
Where is my tongue? Πού είναι η γλώσσα μου; *Poú eínai i glóssa mou?*

Now, my mother's tongue lies in ten years' dust,
and my tongue lies with her turned to rust.

# My Mother at the Well

My mother at the well,
> βρύση νερού
>> who spat at the Italian soldier
>> guarding their water,
Italians, once wily-kind, built schools, hospitals,
spooned their romance language
into juvenile Greek mouths,
>> *una faccia, una razza*
>> one face, one race
they cajoled, then turned black-shirt brutal,
> *signorina, signorina*
calls the Mussolini conscript
to her antelope ankles,

my mother at twelve
all hiss, spit, swipe, claw-tooth girl
fetches the day's water,
the clay jug dents her maiden shoulders
> *signorina, signorina*
he reaches her fleeing back
returns the towel she dropped,

this story she told me my mother, who bore
being fathered then fatherless,
brotherless, war upon war
decades, Germans, Italians,
bombs, spies, hunger,

this mother whom I slated,
my herstory untaught me,
sandwiched between white-bread school books,
the plutocracy of English oiled my mouth,

this mother suckles me strength through my cells,
I embrace her in my dreams;
my body, her body.

# Steeling My Childhood

# Tin-Shed Church

Small, rusted, corrugated iron shack,
tiny windows, served as a church.
Hot like a holy tinny
in the wobble of Australian summers,
chilly as a canister in winter.

Not a white chapel
floating on a cliff's edge,
its lapis dome melting
into the ultramarine Aegean,
but a holy tinny.

The dirt road, pot-holes and clefts
ran to ravines in rain,
our old Ford Anglia slew,
me, pitched, limbs in a scratchy lace dress,
mother's Revlon Red mouth
pressed a thin, red line,
father's seafaring hands
white-knuckled the column gear
like a ship's wheel in an Aegean gale.

Those first few years,
rattling down the unsealed track,
my white leather shoes
crunching the small skirt of gravel
that dressed the wooden steps.
This first Orthodox church in a steelworks town,
packed with young mothers, children,
labourer fathers, sat on Sebel metal chairs,
stoic in polyester-nylon Sunday best,

the onion scent of sweat, perfume, powder,
brewed with frankincense
in a cauldron of congregation skin.

The priest, borrowed from another town,
droned in the dim, smoky space,
his gold-threaded vestments glittered,
the beeswax candles drooped like u-turns
and the inevitable flare of candle flame
in a girl's chocolate toss of hair.

*Poof*, up it went, any given Sunday.

# Bucket of Fish

Through the neighbourhood, my sister and I haul
our bucket of fish, rattle our hand-held brass scale.

Small-town afternoon heat, treeless streets, scoria scintilla,
roads a brûlée of bitumen cook our school shoes.

*Would you like to buy some fish?*
Our voices melt into a singsong duet of new, schoolgirl English.

We zig-zag; the bucket drags, full of boneless fish, pearly, silver slips,
father's faultless fillets, plastic bags slung on the rusted hook.

Blind faces of locked screen doors, hallways exhale
miasma of lard and pork chops. We dance the beggar's shuffle,
foot to foot on blistered, red-painted steps.
*Would you like to buy some fish?*

Young 'New Australians', we walk, hedged by saltbush and red-dirt,
the BHP smelter smokes, a monolith behind us,
small-change chinks in our pockets.

We re-tread our father's road; a boy all ribs and begging-bowl eyes,
plunging through a squall of Nazi bullets, blind in the blue Aegean,
breathless for a can of Spam in a sinking supply boat.
*Would you like to buy some fish?*

# Red Piano Accordion

The bellows of my piano accordion
sweep out then in,
like the pleats of a geisha's fan
and my nubbin breasts
rise and fall with its breath.

Its pearly red carapace
hides half my 10-year-old self,
matches the colour of my face
as his hands tap a minor scale
up my spine in little triplet tests.

Crotchets in my beginner's book
march like grubby child soldiers
on the stave and flag their advance
in simple 3 / 4 time.
I master *My Bonnie* as he fiddles
with the hem of my skirt:

*Dunna ya miss thu rust nahooo,*

he calls in Glasgow brogue
as he plans his secret journey
to the border of my panties.

His expedition aborts as my father's voice explodes
like a buzz bomb into our lounge room,
bounces from the bare shellac floor boards
and muffles into the gold velvet curtains.

Shouting from the kitchen,
the daily, domestic combat
between Mum and Dad punches on.

*Two Tongue World*

Verbal volleys launched over
the red Formica table,
family saints cursed and sandwiched
between roast lamb and tears.

My milky fingers yearn for a piano
a migrant labourer cannot afford,
depress the Bakelite buttons of the bass.
The teacher's liver spotted mitt
slides into my blouse and under
the back of my K-Mart training bra.

I shuffle my shoulders,
hands hostage to music-making,
can't flick off the insect
who irks me this minute
and decades later like
a mosquito-tinnitus
at the slip of slumber.

That red accordion still sits,
glows in my music room.
The sticky-fly teacher whines in memory,
but the accordion sleeps smothered,
its buttons and ivory keys
silent.

# Old Spice

I sit on my bed crying,
red ears flare a testimony to his slap.
My father sits on my bed next to me,
brown palms pressed into his tears.

The fallen bottle of *Old Spice*
I bought him for Father's Day
sobs its innards onto the floor:
father and daughter weep onto the glass.

The alcohol gives up its spirit:
lemon, anise, aldehydes and cedar
expire in piquant resignation,
liquid seeps into cracked lino.

Anger at his money I'd spent,
hard won sweat in dockyards,
earmarked to be sent back home.
Wrath, impotence and regret,
poverty and pressure-cooker shame.

I never saw my father cry
before and never again,
even before his heart stopped.

I remember this now
this sorry, sorry business;
I am sorry I forgot,
he was sorry.

# Grace

Forehead
stomach
right shoulder
heart,
my father's hand
makes the cross.

                      North
        East                        West
                South,

sketched in air
with his right hand,
not the left,
left is the devil's fortress,
women sit on the
left in his church.

Handmade talisman,
in the four directions,
for protection
one for food today,
two for food yesterday,
three for famine remembered
four for emptiness to come.

His hands,
sun and salt-tanned skin,
breaking Australian bread
on a second hand table
in the slum-burbs of
Whyalla,
a steel town.

# Harlot Times Two

## Scream

We lingered
at Death and the Maiden,
Munch's whip-stroke pencil
scratching through the virgin's hair,
and my mother spoke her advice,
a mouthful of bruised trust
I swallowed as if at her breast;
about love,                   un-lasting,
about men,                    faithless,
about our new home,           a catalogue of complaint.

An exhibition of foreign art on this foreign soil,
but she was glad to walk it with me,
her first daughter, 19, the first at university,
   wandering through           a gallery in Terra Nullius,
   Australia,                  the land
   of theft                    and trickle down.

We paced polished floors,
her Greek, dancing,
wild thyme-threshing feet,
and my hybrid soles
that trod her village
only once as a baptised child,
on her white rock
that was raided, robbed and returned.

Every kindness I denied her
screamed into Munch's maw
in that exhibition I took her to,
that 'O', a round grave of mouth and eyes

where all my regrets
fall and echo still.

We walked and watched,
migrants drifting through a gallery
built on stolen soil,
listening to smothered screams.

## Shadow Stain

Shadow-stain,
                forgot you sat,
                              there in my thigh's fat,
and when I       met you again
my petals                          sprang back,
    an effigy                  of my flowering self,
                and I re-heard
my father's words:          *whore, poutana, πουτάνα,*
                            *harlot, porni, πόρνη,*
the daily mantra of         my teenage years.

Rorschach stain,                   like first blood
                bloomed        from virgin veins,
like the spread              across the king-size bed
of he who came,    crowned himself      'husband',
donned the         robe      of honeymoon sheets,
probed my back catalogue
                then proclaimed:
                      *promiscuous.*

That word,       septic     capsule of sin
hatched to             trap   a woman's wildness
              into   a suburban      sty of sound.
That clot of consonants:
                        *promiscuous,*
hurled me time travelling
                      to old Greek mothers,
mumbling black bundles of widows' weeds
                    whose slit-eyes swung
left and right from rigid church pews,

*Two Tongue World*

                    weighed the new nubs
of our sprouting breasts.

Those words,
    sucked me back          into the swallowing stare of men
                whose gaze shucked our pink oysters
    tucked in innocent sleep     beneath white   boyleg pants.

Men        whose eyes              snapped and stored
the Lolita line of lip          and slim, flared hip,
the sheen of our                bared summer skin
                to finger it nightly,
    hands       busy as rock spiders,
between prayer and snoring,     then spat our names
in a stew of spittle   and the stink   of their morning breath.

Those words,                     *poutana, πουτάνα,*
                                      *porni, πόρνη,*
still transmitting
      from a black-hole galaxy       lodged in my cells.

# Curse of Beauty

I remember the curse of beauty
and the armada of eyes that ate me
like acid over a photograph;
men, boys, some women too.

Size ten,
serpentine,
unlined skin

ticked a lot of boxes;
only the blonde box
I did not have

made do with a spill
of bronze-brown gloss
flowing down my back

B-grade, brunette beauty
in an Aussie surf-chick world.

# Cinderella's Zorba

A *Φωτογραφια* of my father sits on the oak dresser in my wood-panelled dining room. *Φωτογραφια* pronounced: 'Fo-to-gru-fee—yu' in Greek, literally means: 'writing with light'. This is a 'light writing' in black and white and grey: a story of my young father, written in shades.

It was taken before he married and well before the sea, salt and diaspora mapped their progress across his face. This is the writing his matchmaking mother sent to my mother's family. This is the shot that bolted into my mother's heart.

His Greek captain's hat is angled, his moustache combed, his shirt, stone-washed white by his mother on Kalymnian rocks, is open necked. His suit jacket, very fashionable in 1950s Europe, would have cost him months of sponge-diver's wages.

His eyes are glossy black, like the little olives he loved to eat. They are hooded; the corners slope downward as he gazes into the lens. His eyes throw light and speak of the mermaid singing. And the mermaids would have gossiped melodiously of my father's love of stylish clothing. He listened to their songs on his many trips between Kalymnos, Piraeus and the Benghazi Coast. His smooth skin is a luminous white, like the moon that tracked his ship's movements across the Mediterranean Sea.

In the bottom right-hand corner of the wooden frame, which houses this light writing, sits another picture of my father. One-eighth the size of its host, it presses into its refuge, fixed there by a grain of BluTack. It is a colour passport photograph. This stamp size shot, snapped on the way home from the Whyalla wharves where he worked as a crane driver; taken just before his one and only return pilgrimage to Greece.

His khaki work shirt, standard issue from BHP, is open at the neck spilling tufts of grey curling hair. His eyes are bleached a fig brown. Red veins travel across the whites and hanging underneath are bladders of skin, melting into his tear troughs. His skin is thick, folded, brown and scribed with wrinkles. This little snap is dog-eared from my handling. Vertical cracks in the paper split his forehead furrows. Horizontal cracks fracture his vertical lines from eyes to mouth. The warp and weft of these broken paper chains cross-hatch and crush his face.

Decades of cigarettes have blued his mouth, but the lips remain large and generous. He attempts a smile. My father was kind, the photographer was innocently doing his job and my father was responsible for his own despair. This is the face, which like Odysseus, he took home. The same face he wore when speaking of the waterfront taverns, turquoise seas and friends of the voyage. This is the face that he screwed into distaste at Australian meat pies and the 'loose' Australian morals I brought home from school.

On the same frame, attached with sticky tape, is a light writing of me. I am at a Greek Orthodox Church dance. I am sixteen, slim and sulking. My hair is a long splice of beach blonde and chocolate brown, parted in the middle in the fashion of the 1970s. My eyelids shimmer with silver shadow, and my lucent lips are a glossy doughnut-frosting pink. My bowling ball heavy head slumps onto my right hand and my eyes search the plastic table-cloth.

A white velvet ribbon, onto which I have tacked a pink fabric rose chokes my throat. My self-sewn dress, of lavender-rose polyester satin, is sliced low on the breast. The bodice undulates across my summer sand-toned décolletage. Long stitches, run through by hand, minutes before the dance began, only just hold the hem together.

This dress turned my father's face red. His mouth spat threats of home detention. He accused me of motives my sixteen-year-old mind could not yet imagine. Our family brawl echoed down the whole Housing Trust street. His verbal blows ricocheted in the old Ford Anglia throughout the jagged journey to the church hall.

As we entered, a gaggle of Greek matrons, moustachioed and blousy-busted, started then turned their backs. Waddling closer to each other, their mouths moved silently beneath the electronic bouzouki music. My father flew from the doorway to the kitchen.

Later that night, I danced the inevitable dance of Zorba. My arms stretched and spread crucifix-like across the shoulders of dancers left and right. Across from me in the circle, men's eyes narrowed and rolled in time with my teenage cleavage. My father's face, eyes down, forehead garlanded in sweat beads, appeared and vanished within clouds of greasy charcoal bar-b-que smoke. Lost and found, like the moon in the clouds that tracked his ship, across the Mediterranean Sea.

# Bravo!

calls my father,
his feet pumping
up the wide, stone smile
of Bonython Hall stairs.

    Μπράβο! *Brávo!*
He grasps my long, white fingers,
piano and student ink,
in his fleshy, fisherman's hands,
browned nacre skin, hook scars
and embossed, tributary veins.

    Μπράβο! *Brávo!*
Flip-flop, my heart fibrillates
beat happy, once, twice
but fails to find
the entrance hall for this word,
a door to let it in.

The rest of our day
is spent wandering,
a nomadic tribe of five
dwarfed amongst campus oaks
that stretch to sweep
an Australian azure sky.

Mother and father squabble,
I stand silent as a Caryatid;
we are borne on the bell
of my graduation robe
ballooning on the summer zephyr.

The photographer lines us up
like an executioner, we press against
thick sandstone university walls
for our one and only family shot.

      *Μπράβο! Brávo! Brávo!*
floats this two-syllable raft
above a decade's dark ocean
of slut-shaming words,
curses and reviling,

      *Μπράβο! Brávo!*
rings through remembered
slaps, spits, knife to my throat,
it tacks like a lifeboat
through roiling storms.

# The Orphaning (ii)

"... between language and body, remembering the past and feeling alive in the present... the body keeps the score."

The Body Keeps the Score, Bessel Van Der Kolk

# The Body Mother Made Me

The body mother made me
                    remembers her.
My lips, her smile stretched across sorrow
and one tooth she lost with each child born.

The body she seeded for me
                    knows her.
Nine moons to grow, twelve more to suck,
years to wean and teethe and cry.

These breasts she planted as buds
                    bloom for her,
flower in my veiled night movements,
swell at full moon with her secret musk.

These feet she fashioned for me
                    danced for her,
in her mountain village square,
stepped the map of her maiden soles.

The hands mother kneaded me
                    labour for her,
pull wild greens, stir her pot,
kindle the lamp of the dead.

This voice she gifted me
                    keens for her,
Doric modes hummed into my breath,
ocean hymns of leaving but always coming home.

These eyes mother lent light to
                    look for her.
My eyes leak her tears now,
now that she is dissolved to bone.

# Aegean Dreaming

### *Sestina for Hands*

Devotional father, I remember your hands
and the prayerful retreat of frankincense.
In your last liturgy you held your saint,
the icon gold upon your unbreathing breast.
Agios Nicholaos, the keeper of seamen,
the saint who heard your mother's prayers.

Your mother wailed the waves with prayers,
stitched spells into nets knotted by your hands,
as you sailed for Benghazi, a boy-child seaman,
clawing you home with candles and frankincense,
through squalling seas, salt on your breast,
she cowed the Aegean with icons of your saint.

Candle heat quivers, melting the eyes of your saint
in this church with the droning dirge of prayers.
His eyes judged my lip-sticked lips and sprouting breast
but never saw the deft slap of your handsome hands,
the council house, the tin-shed church and frankincense
veiling the fading eyes of a married seaman.

In your smooth box with the sunset eyes of a seaman
you lie, forgiven now, resting with your saint.
You navigate the firmament of frankincense,
tanned fingers folded in duty done, and prayer,
your stony hands, still a young man's hands,
cleansed of my teenage tears and sobbing breast.

I shroud my shrunken mother weeping on my breast,
this clever, skilful woman losing her seaman.
Your open coffin displays those woman-hitting hands.

*Two Tongue World*

I light thirty-six candles and kiss your gilded saint,
a diaspora of grey-haired Greeks chant prayers,
my head hovers in rising haloes of frankincense.

From this chanting harbour of candles and frankincense,
I drift into the decade's storms waiting in my breast.
You came and went on waves of wailing prayers,
on the tidal tears of a girl-child seeking her saint.
She found you cowed by campus oaks, a seaman
paying for her English books with night-shift hands.

Frankincense coronas my lost seaman, the hole in
my breast sings sad spells to my saint, candles burn,
and prayers are chanted still to your landlocked hands.

# The Angiogram

Politely
he waited,
he didn't want to fuss,
and pain kept him vigil
as he rubbed his chest
and waited, waited,
politely.

Small man,
survivor of war, fascists
terrifying, three-storey seas,
non-English speaking,
couldn't read the writing
on the doctor's wall,
but knew how to wait
and so waited,
politely.

His first daughter dreamed
he'd hidden his heart
in some shadowed part
of the brown-brick
austerity period house.

Thoughts needled her day:
*to go back to father,*
*take time away*
*from the husband,*
*learn CPR.*
Strange thoughts, uninvited,
three months before.

Three months
he waited and worried,
worried and waited
inching up the waiting list,
he worried politely,
faith in his God,
faith in his doctors.

Practising patience
with a whole village of public patients,
foreign tongues tied to their palates,
ovine eyes skimming old magazines
in the GP's drop-in waiting room
where no appointments
were needed and none were made.

When his heart monitor's
acid green needle
darted upward then sank
like the arc of the diver
he once was in the Aegean,
he glanced up with that captain's gaze
to a sky beyond the hospital ceiling
and advised us politely:
    *I'm going to die.*
    Θα πεθάνω.
    Tha petháno.

The call came two weeks after
the funeral and first tears done,
a cheery nurse's voice
offering his angiogram,
a choice of times,
his number had finally come up.

She stammered her *sorry*,
*he is gone, so sorry*
but not so surprised

then ticked his name off her list,
another one of many so many
waiting,
waiting politely,
for a late offer.

# Cake of the Dead

That druzy dome of icing sugar,
startling white like the
limed cheeks of chapels
that jut, iconic, into the
azure Mediterranean sea:
I want one of those at my funeral.

Beneath this snowy powdered arch
crossed with silver ball sprinkles,
a crumble of boiled wheat, almonds,
parsley and ruby pomegranate;
the blood seed of Persephone's salvage,
her holiday pass out of Hades.

This pagan motif, cooked by a crone
nestles cuckoo on a Christian altar,
mushrooms into memorials.
Anonymous, no sad picture
of the departed servant of God
to whom it is pledged;
the village knows who is gone.

Children crack its sifted cupola,
stuff it into their mouths,
scream through the church yard
laugh and scatter seed,
confirming its immortality.

# Chicken Bones

My widowed mother at lunch
plucks filaments of flesh
from near-naked chicken bones.
She splinters each twig-leg,
vacuums the slurry of marrow:
> They used to hit me.
> Με χτύπησαν. Me chtýpisan.
masticates a small voice
I've never heard before.

She hunches over the fowl's remains,
rounded shoulders, arms over breasts
ball into a child's shield.
Her head twitches like a sparrow's;
left, right, her brown eyes flick up, flick down;
her plastic cataract lenses flash
the phantom of a chthonic hunger.

> They used to hit me. Με χτύπησαν. Me chtýpisan.
> When I went to rock the baby, during the war, they hit me.
> They didn't give me much to eat. I starved,

mewls this babyish voice again,
now from the back seat of my car,
as I chauffeur her from doctor to doctor.

My knuckles whiten on the wheel
like a mottled backbone,
like the mountain range
that splits her island,
as this famishment spools
a spillage of secrets

*Two Tongue World*

so late in life,
like the small, silent histories
of unaccompanied minors,
refugees and war infants;
countless children.

# The Unvisited Graves of Priests

Day's end at the monastery
notched into the mountain.
A novice priest perches on the cliff's edge.
He breathes vespers into the sun soaked sea.
At the last second of sunset the sea liquefies
into a sheet of rippling gold leaf.

The peacocks caw all day from the *nekrotafeío*,
their tails a crowd of blind blue eyes.
The peacocks call and bob amongst the crosses
and sterile graves of priests.

The unvisited graves of priests trouble me in my sleep,
their dove grey marble pristine from the tears
or wet good-bye kisses of unborn children,
the bodily leaking of love in grief.
I worry my death too will be mourned only by birds.

The sea of Corfu is a quivering mosaic
of emerald, turquoise and lapis,
white lace nerves of light split in water,
its sleepy *shush—shush* slips into my ears.

Below at the café,
playing chess with my new young friend,
he moves his King into my Queen's path;
check-mate: he is much younger than me.

Fishermen stand next to their
cyan blue boats
knitting the holes in their nets.

All this will re-orphan me, when I leave again.

# Wick

My aunt's words cut the afternoon light,
horizontal palm, a hand-knife
slices air viscous with olive oil,
in her chicken-coop flat,
windows small as a ship's
frame the sepia clouds of Athen's smog.
>	*Up to there his candle burned.*
>	Μέχρι εκεί έκαψε το κερί του.
>	*Méchri ekeí ékapse to kerí tou.*

Her guillotine chops the head
from my gluey sentiment,
cultured in English literature books
and university halls.

The first breath you draw
kindles your wick;
your soul flares
and so your candle burns
its allotted time.

Here are life's lessons
through a child's eyes
educated on decades' diets
of occupation, struggle,
bullets and never enough.

No more talk or weeping about
her brother freshly buried,
gone from his home over 30 years,
his photograph, an ageless,
migrated shadow
but for the unfailing remittances.

The tears I carefully packed
and stored on the long-haul flight
from Australia freeze-dry in my ducts,
shoved back into my baggage,
I stop sobbing;
his candle burned to here.

# Hymn of Belonging

# Earth My Body

### I

Earth my body,
makings from dirt,
sweat and dark night cries

you thrum, octaves deep
earth my body sleeps,
a chthonic heartbeat

clan sealed in cells,
earth my body coded
to slot back here

sod sings to skin,
breathes wild thyme,
earth my body

### II

feet greet sand, white-rock spine,
when I land sea-soaked
the soil kens the mould of me

familiar too the old olives
whose roots knit friendship
in filaments through clay

at day's dissolve
they tell each other stories
of birds' return, sun and fruit

I hear them hum
my mother tongue
into the rising mist

### III
home, to re-knit
my scattered puzzle
of borrowed bones

blue-print covenant,
blood-debt webbed
in ossein honeycomb

pilgrimage to repay
this land's lending-tax
with lotic tears

earth my body-memory
makings from dirt,
sweat and dark night cries.

# Greece

## A Quintet

jade, turquoise, lapis
ganglia of trembling light
the ocean of Greece

sap of cypress pine
redolent glue on fingers
scent travels with me

goat-bell sonata
a jingling scale, up, then down
the clef of Mount Athos

a clutch of nuns chant
vespers in lengthening light
Saint Nicholaos

twist of olive trees
ancient clan at day's dissolve
twine roots, hum language

# Whose Are You

                                               ποιανού είσαι; *poianoú eísai?*
they ask my suit-case stranger's face
as I drop, from the bus's mouth
into a lime-washed village square
sluiced in midday sun.
                                       Ποιανού είσαι; *poianoú eísai?*

chime these elderly twins,
their bi-focal glasses telescope
a black eyeball of Greek Chorus?
                       Not: *What's your name,* but: *whose are you?*

My surname is the blank envelope
I arrive in. My mother's maiden name,
matrilineal uttering, an offer
fresh from her new grave:
                                     Επιτροπούλου, *Epitropoulou,*
their faces flap open like ledgers,
lips like bookmarks spill my lineage,
intone generations of oral DNA;
no scratchings on paper.

                 Yes, *whose am I?* Ποιανού είμαι; *Poianoú eímai?*
my parents' bones interred
in *Terra Nullius*, accidents of migration,
geographies of unspoken theft,
twenty-eight stormy, flying hours away.
                                             *Whose am I,*
nesting on this sage-scented eyrie?
Hellenic keys still charm the lute's strings
and blonde-haired, blue-eyed girls
rebut the Ottoman's clutch.

*Two Tongue World*

                                  *Whose am I ? Ποιανού είμαι;*

I am my mother's child.
My *wog* pariah rags transform
into a Goddess' gown
and I attend the ball.

All night my aunts' hands
plaited across each other's breasts,
legs spring to the hiccupping 7/8 beat,
the blood-thick wine
spooned into their mouths
fuels the mantra of their feet.

Hours pass the midnight hours
in the church courtyard
where the figs fruit fat
on that ageless, spreading tree
that once fed my grandmother
and now feeds me.

Dancers link, coil, bob as one body
on the hypnotic pulse,
spiral like ribbons from the double helix
threading my story through theirs.

                                    *Whose are you? Ποιανού είσαι;*
                                    The hymn of belong,

                                    belong,

                                    belong.

# Arachne's Thread

Her hands made this
whose hands I never knew,
whose hands I'll never know,
whose skull lies, clean, cool
and catalogued in an ossuary
where I will likely never go.

Great aunt Sophia,
her sepia-shadowed face
in hooded nun's habit
her only photograph,
spinning, weaving, sewing
my grandmother's trousseau.

Arachne's thread,
her dynasties of doilies,
ladder-lace land
like my genes purling,
knit red by mother
and slipknot black by father.

Nailed to my cottage wall
in an Australian *burb*
her white weaving
spins our stories.
Skeins kiss then part,
re-twine and plot our decades
through diaspora's winds.

Unschooled these literacies in linen,
'unqualified' women's arts,
cohorts soundless
as their arachnid sisters.
Women's hands, patient,
deft and endlessly useful.

My fingertips decrypt
family narratives in fibrous braille,
travel her spidery, red cross-stitch,
my grandmother's virgin name
needled like nuptial blood
on bridal sheets.

Long-line weft of war and want,
warp of small church steeples,
pucks, patterns, tensile pulse
she loomed and trapped in cloth.

# Dogolalia

Do dogs in Greece bark in Greek?
Aesop did not say.

Lick-lick-lick, is glossolalia
as dogs belong you in many tongues.

Drool means wet, generally,
cringe-worthy in most countries.

Howl is Wolvine polyglot,
piercing the globe with the call to nest.

Twitch-dream paws are mute Morse
for twilight pack hunts of hapless prey.

Snarl is pearl-flash, fang-lingo for
submit, belly-up or throat offer.

But smell – smell is all languages,
universal syntax for food, mate, friend or foe.

Odour –   the canine code of order:
          Butt-sniffling protocols,
          Sniff-trails, collecting and leaving
          secret, silent 'pee-mail',
          maps for roaming and homing
          unknown to human snouts.

And home – home is where we
bark, lick, drool, howl, twitch, snarl and sniff,
                              together.

# Little White House
## *Memory is a Sea of Myth*

My mother said that when we left for Australia, I threw the ball from the plane to my cousin Vasili and he threw it back to me in a final game of 'catch'. I was two and a half; he was five and lived next door to our house at Yiannou Svorounou 21 in Piraeus. Now, I wonder how an infant could throw a ball from the sealed window of an aeroplane. Did we instead play that game in the courtyard of our little white house? Play together, before the taxi took us to Athens airport, where we climbed into the belly of the giant, bug-eyed, iron beast that would fly us to Australia, Melbourne, Adelaide, and then finally to the vast red earth, saltbush deserts of Whyalla.

My Grandfather Yiannis built that little white house in Piraeus. 'Pappous', the Greek word for Grandfather, was a tough old man with sunburned leathery skin and pronounced cheekbones. He was tall for his generation; wiry and mother said he was a good dancer. He survived the Great Depression, lasted the Great Famine in Athens during the war but death finally snared him at the age of ninety-six with a simple fall.

Grandfather Yiannis, a native of the island of Karpathos, laboured for decades as a guest worker in Persia. Mother said that a blind elder in her village foresaw the migration of youth to the cities; her generation obliged to leave their island homes for work and marriage. The village formed a collective and grandfather bought land in Piraeus with the money he earned. The suburb was walking distance to the port and was once the haunt of refugees of the exodus from Asia Minor. Heroin and prostitute dens, taverns playing Rembetika, the Greek blues: a resting place for the dispossessed. Over time, a 'respectable' population from the Aegean displaced these unlucky nomads and it became Kallipolis: or 'good city'. The land and house were my mother's dowry and she resisted signing it over to us, right up to the year before her death.

Grandfather worked away in Persia for a year at a time, for there was no real living to be made on the island in the 1920s. He would return home, sire another daughter and depart again to toil for the dowry money that Greek tradition demanded the bride bring to the marriage. My grandmother's life was a rotation of gestation, breastfeeding and raising her five children—husbandless.

Chrisanthi, whose name means 'golden blossom', was a widow with a daughter when she married Yiannis. In Chrisanthi's time, widows rarely remarried. Only the rich or the very beautiful won another chance. Ordinary women, trudged through the remainder of their days, draped in black and heads bent, attending their husbands' graves.

Our family has two photographs of Chrisanthi. A Greek woman of her generation merited a photograph only once: on her wedding day, when the transfer of her ownership from father to husband justified the cost of the photographer. The rare second picture happened in the courtyard of *her* little white house in Karpathos at a time close to her death and my mother's departure for the mainland. My grandmother's Parkinson's had progressed and she sat surrounded by her children. Her hands, curled into stiff claws, rested in her lap. Her lips stretched and seemed to tremble beneath Greta Garbo cheekbones. Her beauty had fled into her eyes from where it flashed with something I judged to be stoicism, or acceptance—a quiet courage.

It's the same smile, I imagine, that my mother wore as she knelt before the train, 35 years after that flying machine funnelled us into an industrial town, along with the myriads of migrants who fed the smelters of BHP steelworks. I imagine it, because the witnesses in the coroner's report did not mention it; but I sense it was there, as my mother wore that smile daily. It was her constant accessory as she saw me off to school, as she welcomed me home, as she sat at the red Formica kitchen table day in day out. This smile remained fixed on her lifeless face, under the downlights in the mortuary: a final punctuation mark of her disappointment in this diaspora.

My grandmother's little white house in her village, Othos, Karpathos still stands. From my mother's perch in the courtyard, I looked down the mountain to see ferries sail into the harbour and main town, Pigadia. I watched in peacetime, but she observed the unfolding massacre at the end of the war, when the retreating Nazi Air Force bombed homebound troop ships packed with surviving Italian soldiers.

But our little white house in Piraeus is now a 'Polikatikia'. It means, literally, 'many living'. After mother's death, we sold the house for block value only, to a developer. Many strangers live there now in the erected multistorey apartment building.

When I returned to Greece, in 1999, to see my mother's remaining family, I saw a few little white houses. They pined between the shadows of pastel pink, yellow and grey high-rise apartments. I stared through the fence grates at the blood-heads of poppies in the silent courtyards of Greeks abroad, who neither lived in their homes nor sold them.

As I stood staring at these little houses, the few fragile memories from my infancy materialised. It was less a memory, more my adult body's sensation. I seemed to recall the internal courtyard of our home, its brilliant white in the midday sun. Grandfather built it on traditional Dodecanese architectural lines and so the house had no hallway.

All the rooms opened into the courtyard. We crossed this little courtyard, snow-blanket winter or simmering summer, on our way to a bedroom, the basic bathroom or the kitchen.

The kitchen was the magnetic centre of our home. We were all drawn there, especially when my father, a professional fisherman, returned from his sea voyages, carrying baskets of silver fish, crabs, and spiny sea urchins like pin cushions. Aromas of olive oil, onion, garlic and seafood, from a giant blackened frying pan fanned by the wind ushered me to the wooden table. I was still in nappies, my fat little thighs bare. When I climbed onto the ladder-back chairs with straw woven seats, the backs of my thighs chafed: this itch pricks me even now.

These scents, the chafing, the sneezing of my grandfather who lived with us and my reply, 'Giassoú pappoús', 'Bless You, Grandpa', are little dots. Today, if I sit with bare thighs against a straw woven chair, or smell seafood frying, the picture populates pixel by pixel. It is like remembering a dream. You only need to grasp one detail for it all to unfold.

# Two Tongue Love

# Father Refound

When I met you again after you died,
Dear Father, you were no apparition,
your fig-brown gaze now glittered blithe blue eyed,
your child-starved bones a Titan rendition.
Sharp Greek words hushed, now a lush Irish lilt
danced bird-song sorcery upon his tongue,
still the Siren's call to broken bonds fit
grooves you cut through my heart when I was young.
So handsome, you both, like old photographs
when the white sclera of your seaman's eyes
flagged the new moon in the mast and the laugh
lifting your youthful mouth, a beggar's prize
to a child's eyes burned bitter by water,
in vigil for love, a landlocked daughter.

# Eyes like Black Plates

Talk and touch and touch and talk and in the dark, eyes like black plates,
I hear my breath rattle in the rock-rock cradle of his arms,
and a fit so simple, like the sigh of 38 year's wait.

Fit and scent and scent and fit and sounds with words that vibrate
in the flutter of my breath in the rock-rock cradle of his arms,
talk and touch and touch and talk and in the dark, eyes like black plates.

Sound and sigh and belly on thighs and his push-push rock placates,
and little mewling mantra love sounds rise, lilt and charm,
and a fit so simple, like the sigh of 38 year's wait.

Siesta arrives, the village sweats, moans and gyrates,
lust sifts through curtains, coats the priest's ears waking him in alarm,
talk and touch and touch and talk and in the dark, eyes like black plates.

White sheet and sun and all our inside skin turned to touch its mate,
my face buried in nesting folds of neck, held tightly from harm,
and a fit so simple, like the sigh of 38 year's wait.

Sea shush, olive trees susurrate and the breeze sings the gate,
shadows splayed and shuddering on the blue walled shuttered farms,
talk and touch and touch and talk and in the dark, eyes like black plates,
and a fit so simple, like the sigh of 38 year's wait.

# Τρυφερός

red poppy sieves
winter sun

                        *tryferos*
                        τρυφερός

teeth bite into
inner skin

                        τρυφερός

lover shapes
my mouth

                        τρυφερός

fingers search
brown skin

                        τρυφερός

# Fruit of Exile

Sweet fruit of exile,
ripe and splitting
with the seed of memory,
want of home,
and pining
for kin, hearth and heart.
Sweet fruit soft with hope
of forgetting.

To find you here;
marvellous strange fruit,
the wind in your hair,
the blossom's wind
in your lovely hair.

What twisted paths
my feet have trod,
mountain tracks thick with vines,
roads wet with infant sorrow
and long, long goodbyes.

What twisted paths
my feet have trod,
to crush eucalypt
underfoot with you,

learn to cherish
your weathered face,
your broken mended face,
and forsake my cross and master.

Lost fruit of homeland,
wandering seed,
nomad's hands unraveling roots,
moving onward,
moving.

Sweet fruit of exile,
ripe and splitting.
Sweet fruit,
soft fruit, soft with hope,
sweet, sweet, fruit.

# Rachmaninov's Vespers

I am newly returned from my pilgrimage to Greece, searching my mother's roots: looking for her in her sisters' faces, the thyme studded sod she trod, the streets she ran through as a child and the well where spat at the Italian soldier.

Fragments are all I found: oral histories told by the Hapsis twins, the gimlet gaze of my Aunt Irini whose eyes my mother wore. Small stories remembered by relatives; the foreign yet familiar feel of a never-met family, pressed from the same clay. DNA mirrors, walks and talks, a queer and comforting feeling. Still, their scraps soothed my starvation; gave me something I could cling to that said she was once happy.

You collect me from the airport. My Greek summer body, amber nacre skin in a white dress glows in your antique Saab. Your lust speaks in hand questions, renewed from the chastity of my six-month absence, but I put it on pause this first night as we attend Rachmaninov's Vespers in the Catholic Cathedral in Flinders Street.

Layers upon vocal layers of bass, embroidered with soprano and the critical middle layer of the sandwich, the altos who do all the blending work but receive little praise. I think how I hate singing alto and bristle if I, a dramatic soprano, am pinned there.

It is September 1999 and our future is still a seesaw of your ambivalence and my reactive insecurity. What is clear is that you want me, at least my body, you along with all other men I have known desire me with some sort of rare frenzy. You cannot cope with my intensity vertical but horizontal, the sheets absorb your doubts.

Our ears still soaked with worship of the Rach, we begin the bonding of breath, breast, buttock, cleft and rut. In my bowels the bass, the alto, my mouth lifts with the float of the soprano as you glide. It is a depth charge of moan, wrestle and friction. The spasm arrives and its tandem endorphin flood melts me into a soul-travel sleep. The Dalai Lama says death and orgasm are the same. Our bodies wrap supple as rubber; inner skin of wrists, thighs, kiss each other.

Then, in that hypnogogic state, she arrives. Nothing from her for 18 months; she has been a poor correspondent from the world beyond. She, who in body stalked me from room to room in our Housing Trust house and later by phone after I escaped to university. The random current of loin and lip wired into the music to conduct her ethereal note. She, the astral traveller, spiritual sender, gut feelings like a flick-knife, blade out, slicing through dross. Nothing: I have pined and pined, but a haze of silence persisted. A suicide I am told takes time to heal. Her soul has been in the angels' repair shop in a parallel dimension divided by a meniscus like the skin of a tear: thin but not porous.

Then after Rachmaninov, the dissolving sex, my surrendered sleep, my mother runs down the corridor to my bed and presses her forehead to mine. It is visceral; not a dream, this child's way of connecting. I see it hundreds of times in schoolyards as I do yard duty.

"I'm sorry," she osmotes in this liminal space because spirits have no vocal apparatus. Her words steep into my cells. The small bones of my ears receive her apology and drum happiness.

"Don't be sorry mum," I osmote back in English, in life we spoke only Greek, my mother tongue, "I'm so glad to see you." When I awake the next morning, my heart beats spaces like semibreves with rests between them.

# Tongue Song for Women

# Washing

On the rocks the women are singing,
slapping their sheets to free the night's stains,
saliva, blood and seed into water;
in my bones their song remains.

My grandmother's face, father's mother,
business brow and no-nonsense mouth,
sloe eyes that calculate the last
shred of bread on a child's plate;
stamped in my cells, her songs' refrains.

Through my mother's smile
long, laboured in mourning,
island notes twirl into foreign air,
in household chores and daily duties,
though there was no audience to hear.

On her, the childbearing burden lay,
her fat, my fat, lost and regained,
storehouse of centuries, hedge against famine;
in bowls of breasts, hips and buttocks
this song sustains.

On the rocks the women are singing,
slapping their sheets to free the night's stains,
saliva, blood and seed they are kneading;
in my bones, sinew, fat, their song remains.

# Woman is the Cow of the World

Udder and tit, meat and trade she is it, picked over and laid,
everyday chattel and like her pretty sister, cattle,
she is driven, riven, ploughed, sucked, trafficked and trucked,
                    woman is the cow of the world

Labia majora razored to minor, surgically sculpted little girl flowers,
cut for Web porn, doctors define her, uploaded midnight to dawn hour by hour
hopeful checkout chick splayed on the casting couch of lick-dick,
revolver between her tits, up her vulva, princess of gun pornography,
her body a cartography of man's squirt and grunt,
                    woman is the cow of the world

Pressed mute in pages of the Bible, on the left side of churches,
swept from priestess to prostitute by a scratch of Pope Gregory's pen,
holy oracle to hole, abbess to scrubber in the Magdalen laundries,
vessel of God to unwed mother-bitch, healer to stripped, scorched witch,
                    woman is the cow of the world

Woman is the tart with or without heart, the whore with more on all fours
waste of space when her dugs stretch to the floor, jiggling milk in lap dance
blue-veined jugs, nipple frothing under lace, aching to feed an infant mouth
in need at home alone,
                    woman is the cow of the world

Woman is the pack-animal lugging water, dung and her family honour,
black burqa spectres with letter box faces, amber eyes written in khol,
mailing panicked messages, sisters snuffed-out by silk pillows squashed
in the mitts of her brothers who creep away lawless as shadows
to pray at the mosque beside her unnamed lover,
                    woman is the cow of the world

Woman is the bleeder, the breeder, the walking womb sperm bank
with no Super-scheme, penned quietly in suburban nurseries,
babbling to babies, losing her place in the money race,
losing her figure then her mind,
                    woman is the cow of the world.

## Two Tongue World

...urdered wives, uncounted each week, by the loves of their lives, corpses
...n't speak of pets butchered in practice runs, children's bodies hung
...n their breasts with the sob frozen on their last breath, so few arrests,
                              woman is the cow of the world.

...ar-raped, sown on mass with soldiers' seed so her newborns' faces
...ag her captors' races and tap her labour, horizontal slavery,
...cund engine pumping generations of battle butchered boys.
...o, not news. But true, today as always,
                    woman,    is,            the cow of the world.

# The Offering

Rosa Grandiflora,
giant head thrust over a fence, black-red felt,
pop-out gift card, canes a ligature of thorns.

She is sprung,
splayed for any passing eye, nose, hand,
seeks the drone, sucks the sun.

Her sillage
rides the Levant winds,
would saturate a small room.

Labyrinth folds
conceal-reveal a filament heart,
occult ovary, lancing stigma.

Her scent,
lemon, musk, bottomless amber,
argot of rose catalogues and wine snobs.

Comparison,
the uncourted guest uploads
lightning luggage to my synapses

O'Keefe's water-colours,
altar of labial blooms, a colossal soft assault,
pleated promise, ruching ready to unfurl.

I segue
into aroma, the social slander of smell,
tango of lust with disgust.

Tangled lexicon
of origami mystery that could rescue
her olfactory name.

Clean
viscous albumen, watered civet,
cedar, organic mushroom mulch.

Oceanic,
sea urchin flesh dissolved,
split by tongue on a boat in Crete,

earth met sea,
jolt of pheromone orgy, salt, sandalwood
midnight sweat, married in a Mediterranean storm.

# Coffee Cup

> Come, I will tell you your coffee.
> Έλα να σου πω τον καφέ σου,

calls the clairvoyant, hair in Medusa ringlets,
her eyes a laser of hazel, long, brown fingers,
her grandmother's gift, twirl my little cup.

My lips siphoned coffee; breathed shapes into life,
dot-painting portents lace my demitasse,
sylphs fly in this tiny cauldron only she can scry.

Whispers and giggles in kitchens across Greece:
secret women's business flout the priest's commands
to deny this pagan sin, forgo this women's knowing.

A sea of symbols speaks in sticky Turkish coffee
tattles my tales: marriage, children to come, lucky money,
splotches of sickness, but cats' bodies uncurl jealousies.

Bird wings augur mail that always comes,
handwritten in my mother's time, now it might be email;
a fleck of Facebook spite, a spot of Tweet gossip.

So much news in this mystical miniature
map of mud, my universe-to-be logged
in the bottom of my small, bone china cup.

# Thirteen Ways of Looking at a Fig

on spring's bare boughs
first figs sprout, tight
as boys' new testicles

late summer figs
weep milk and
viscous sugar tears

the poet's hands
spill twelve figs into
my palms' chalice

hollow of flowers
pollen death pact
for love struck wasps

crimson heart shapes,
calyx constellations,
petals tangled like love

revelation of ovaries,
florets, vulva's sister,
just rude fruit

split, succulent vug
tugs my tongue into
its wild, red womb

siko, fico, la figue,
el higo, die Feige,
figging in tongues

purple pendant bruise,
skin burst surrender
to hunting teeth

half-open, an umbrella
green ribs wait
for saliva to rain

fig's mother of mothers
fruited in Eve's mouth,
the apple was a typo

Jesus struck and cursed
the barren fig tree,
Judas hung himself there

black figs, olives, bread
on Lent's pink full moon,
my mother's table, my table

# Three Dips

### *i Tarama Dip*
*Taramosalata*

I watch my mother torment diced onion with a fork,
pressing its pearly mosaic into red cod's roe.
Slow work, like her mother and mother and mother
before her. I, the clever daughter, blitz *my tarama* in the blender,
parade the pink dip in a glass-artist, mouth-blown bowl.
Still, hers tastes deeper, each ingredient presents itself,
talks of turquoise seas, the fish and its hooked regret,
long Lenten fasts broken after midnight mass.
This alchemy of scent, sight and salt travels time.

### *ii Tomato Salsa*
*Tomatosalsa*

My mother's knife bites a cross into tomato skin,
peels it back, the way the Ottomans skinned Greek rebels
alive in village squares, exposing the fascia, jewelled
carmine flesh, translucent. She cuts her victims into four,
eight, luminous cubes, pushes them through the *mouli*
which migrated with us and sweats tomatoes on a heat so low
the flame whispers the fruit of its soul. I, the daughter
who won the school English prize, pulse my canned tomatoes
through the processor, slap them into the frying pan,
hot as hell it spits and carps. At the table hers confesses its biography:
the soil it grew in, the sun's caress and the bees' courtship.

### *iii* **Garlic Dip**
*Skordthalia*

My mother pounds an industrial amount of garlic
with a split piece of wood, half an old wooden spoon
broken when she smacked my rebellious bottom.
The cloves' maimed membranes submit to her savagery
that plugs on until the kitchen funks sulphur,
caustic and viscous with the odour of allium abuse.
Then a tumble of boiled potatoes; pummel, thrash, thump.
Next, the silent, green cascade of virgin olive oil
until the white, dip drifts thick on crusty bread,
violent, pungent but vegan virtue on yet another religious fast.
I, the published daughter, submit my garlic to the Nutriwhizz,
mud-slide of potatoes and oil sucked into the stainless steel vortex.
My efficiency fluffs peaks and hollows, but my drift is wan snow.

I remember her hands in all these actions;
her recipes written in primary school Greek,
in a tongue whispered in secret moonlight schools,
occupation after occupation. I, the digitised daughter,
type my recipes in English, broil them in Microsoft's blue-light zone,
but they have no smell.

# Through the Mouth

Driving home I see new oranges
swelling on the neighbour's tree
and I remember my mother

threading orange skin onto cotton string,
a lei of little rolled peels
plunged into the boiling jam pot,
chemistry of sugar and citrus, yielding
that sticky spoon sweet we stole

peeling, rolling, piercing the pith,
her needle blinked in nimble fingers
her hands a brown crosshatch of cuts
from cleaning purslane, chicory,
dandelion; liver loving greens
Anglo-Australians called *weeds*.

Glacé peel she gave to guests,
on a tiny cut-crystal dish,
jewelled marmalade married
the demitasse of Turkish coffee mud,
and a tall glass of iced water

served on a Ranleigh steel tray,
on a warm afternoon after siesta,
in that space before night's demands,
her smile mirrored up at her,

I remember her through my mouth,
the way most Greeks take in the world,
not by eye, or ear,
but through the mouth.

# Epilogue

*This is my testimonio and memoir as I remember it.*
*All memory is a sea of myth.*
                              Maria Koukouvas

# Babel Box

The Migrant Resource Centre
is a busy box of Babel,
a begging bowl blur of traffic;
bewildered people in need
of work, a smile, electricity,
an oracle to decipher
the runes on a speeding fine,
a doctor who can stomach
the carrion of genital mutilation
or stop the rape baby growing.

A Kandinsky of colour flies
in and out the front door,
a swish of loud dyed silks,
beaded saris and red turbans,
a clutch of black-veiled women
ghosting in silence, the habit
of waiting kohled in their eyes,
a cassoulet of spiced skin,
street-huddles of girls giggling
sofa lips and smart phones,
dark chocolate bellies
blinging taboo piercings.

All the Englishes blend piquant
creoles in the Babel box,
a curry of tongues and a cacophony
of vowels and consonants to rival
Shostakovich's Symphony No. 10
E minor with its industrial grind.

All diasporas are the same,
whatever lingo you flap;
maelstroms of migrations
to this wide, red land,
*Terra Nullius.*
We are twisted and racked
between exodus and entry,
refugee visa in one hand,
title to stolen land in the other.

    *You Greek, you Greek?*
    *Eísai Ellinas?*
    *Είσαι Έλληνας;*
prods my mother of every
olive-skinned stranger at her bus stop,
    *You Italian? You Vietnamese, Sudanese?*
    *You speeka da Eeennglleesh?*

The perennial split
in my mind and tongue,
the two-ness of heart,
the gap between
my *new Australian* face
and theirs will never close,
my race will never quite melt
into the mythical, multi-cultural
Holy Grail of Australia.

I may chance sea or roar through sky,
but the *good-bye* on my lips
is my forever luggage,
the law of purgatory, daily packing rituals
and fantasies of return.
My home, the longing,
my new home, relief and hope,

*Two Tongue World*

the othering in this stranger's place,
the gathering with ex-pats, whose class
I could never meet back home.

All diaspora's children
wear the same mantle
of schizophrenia and shame,
our names an Anglicized scribble,
a teacher's roll call fumble,
that dices with dialects
and phonic disgrace.

I am ripped roots and scattered seed.
I am other, othered and othering,
hunting peace my swinging pendulum soul
on the tightrope of identity
until I am *naturalised*,
hybridised,
until I forget.

# Space and Wind

### Watervale Clare Valley 19.10.2019

Walking the fields and streets of Watervale, with my dogs Duke and Oonah. Arching canes of wild roses, abandoned churches, burnt-gold fields of barely grass. The dogs pluck and smell their way through. Grape vines crawl like cornrow hair styles across soft slope after slope.

Duke prances up the stairs of St Mary's church like he's going to pray with those Jack Russell paws. His orange coat and jewelled collar glow against the distressed green door. Oonah looks up, down and around; she, my sable, abandoned Shar Pei, still seeks her God.

The streets are wide; so wide the wind of desolation needs to puff up to fill them as it whines through: its song is loneliness. Suddenly I remember this wind trailing me to school, daily through the cavernous, treeless streets of Whyalla, as I squinted into the sun.

In my parents' villages, the streets are thin ribbons cut into rock and ragged mountains facing the Mediterranean Sea. The blue eye of the bay looks up and beguiles the bleached cottages. The slim streets hold them, fitted like a corset. Tight places, like tight families: too close for middle class Western culture: 'co-dependent' the psychologists label this densely taut-laced kinship.

The streets are a firm embrace in Greece, in France, in Italy and Spain. Here in Watervale the wide, empty streets of country Australia offer a loose welcome. Handsome, old houses rise from expansive sandstone stairs that lead to mute mouthed front doors, heavy with oak and jewelled with stained glass.

The desolation of Whyalla stays with me and I understand what led my mother to Valium. Wind, wind, wind, salt-bush, rust-red earth, spreading open streets, no extended family. I am a small student, just five years old, picking my way over stones, the wires strung on Stobie poles, whine a daily lament. Everything is too big. It swallows me. That moaning draught drove students to misbehave and their graduate teachers to impotent threats in chaotic, mixed race classrooms.

Whyalla, the industrial town packed full of migrants and their families. Imported armies of labour, funnelled into the BHP steelworks whose smoke stack bilged and presided obelisk-like above the main street. It took me decades and years of writing to understand, the wives and children were surplus to requirements so the schools, hospitals and other infrastructure provided was minimalist.

In my mother's village in Karpathos, the lanes almost hugged me as I passed. Space only for a couple of people, a cart or donkey. A road that hosted car tyres and tourist traffic pushed through the main street. Every other path was a cubist fantasy rising into the mountain mist; a narrow path for foot or hoof.

The Dodecanese houses enclose a courtyard. The bedrooms, sofan[2], only allow sleeping packed together like pencils in their box. All of this of course is historical and an architectural necessity. Courtyards, entered from lace iron, street-front doors enfold rooms in a u-shape. The courtyard prevents or retards assault to the guts and heart of a house: safety from intruders, pirates, Ottoman Turks; it gives time to escape. Greece was prey to many occupations over the centuries, including colonisation by Turkey, Venice, Italy, Germany and others. Small and rocky, so flat space was precious: you can't do urban sprawl on a mountainous island. Topography shapes architecture everywhere.

---

[2] *an elevated, sleeping platform in traditional Dodecanese houses*

In Australian suburbs, Port Noarlunga my now home, the shopping malls vomit vast wastelands of carparks without a scrap of green space. This southern jewel with its tidal reef has been discovered by developers who dump cheap townhouses onto shore and into bushland un-homing the remaining wildlife. Our icon, the koala chews into its short future and the eucalypts susurrate a requiem into the buzz of the chain saw.

On my last trip to the village, my aunt jumped into bed with me uninvited the first night I arrived. This is how they all slept as children. I was in my mother's birth-place, my grandmother's death place. Boundaries were familial and instantly intimate. Privacy, not known and only given in certain behaviours, politeness and protocols. Not through physical space. The wind whirls here too but through the slender flute of streets, it's a different song.

# Author's Notes

A book grows organically through the generosity of many people and sources. For my friends in poetry who critiqued my poems, thank you for your honesty and encouragement. Ochre Coast Poets' David and Veronica Cookson; Tess Driver; Virgil Goncalves; Martha Landman; Geoff Aitken; Mike Riddle; Vladimir Lorenzin; Tony King; Murray Alfredson; Diane Wahlheim; Mark Ritchie; Christabel Gollop; Elizabeth Heij and the late Vivien Wade. To Chaos & Critique poets, Ines Marrasso and Shaine Melrose, thank you for those fearless critiquing sessions. I acknowledge the early appraising and support of Trams End poets Dr Lindy Warrell, Nigel Ford, Maria Comino, Valerie Volk and David Harris.

Thank you to those who edited and re-edited evolving versions of my manuscript. In particular, Julia Wakefield's professional and precise eye, blunt feedback, friendship and collaboration in poetry, community workshops and a decade of running an open mic, Southern Performers Interactive Network has been priceless in my poetic development. Julia is a gifted writer and artist whose support is invaluable. Dr Steve Evans also contributed early edits of the manuscript.

I cut my poetic teeth at Friendly Street Poets open mic which has run for over 40 years. For a new poet, Friendly Street offers a supportive, but robust literary environment and it is often where many poets are first published.

I am enriched by the long-term musical collaboration and learning through Dr Demeter Tsounis whose deep knowledge of Greek musical culture and democratic sharing of her virtuoso musicianship has informed many of the poems in this book. Music and poetry share rhythmic roots and I hope music is clearly heard in many of the poems, particularly through depictions of dance; a kinetic history of many migrant and Indigenous cultures.

The cover art, Dancers, is a painting by award winning artist Desma Kastanos, a dynamic, rich and iconic image of dance as cultural heritage. Thank you for enhancing the book with your skilful work.

I am indebted to the talented Dr Rachael Mead for her mentoring and review and my friend in poetry Juan Garrido-Salgado for his review and role-modelling of the powerful, political expression and liberation good poetry creates. Jelena Dinic's reading and support of my manuscript was insightful and helpful as we share a migrant and refugee history: her book *In the Room with the She Wolf* inspired me.

I am surprised and relieved that Howard Firkin, editorial director of ICOE chose to publish my manuscript and endured my fascination with the cosmetics of book covers and poetic pedantry.

For the opportunities of education this new land brought, through Gough Whitlam's vision, I was the first in my family to go to university, I am grateful.

I acknowledge that my family migrated to Whyalla, the lands of the Barngarla people. Today, I live, write on unceded Kaurna land. The nexus between migrant peoples fleeing their indigenous lands and settling the lands of other indigenous peoples is another question growing in my consciousness.

As a mature woman, I feel an overwhelming thankfulness to my parents for keeping our Greek culture and mother tongue alive with all its richness. The schism, tension and complexities this brought us as children growing up in an industrial town and a two-tongue world was unbearable at times, however the remaining cultural capital is indestructible and nourishing.

Finally, to my mother, her oral story telling culture which lead her to never stop telling us stories of her life. Humans are story telling creatures and the stories of refugees, migrants, migrant children and their contributions to our country must be told and retold.

# About the Author

Maria Koukouvas (formerly Maria Vouis) is a Greek migrant. The schism of a two-tongue world fuels her poems. She writes about children in care, the voicelessness of animals, Indigenous issues, refugees and other minorities. Maria is a registered teacher and teaches Life Writing, Poetry, English, and Literacy. She lives by the sea on Kaurna country with her two dogs Duke and Pax.

Maria won the Satura Prize for 'Sepia apama' and the manuscript prize for Friendly Street New Poets 19. Her work features in journals, newspapers and books including: *The Saltbush Review*; *Cordite, Canberra Times*; *Newcastle Poetry Prize*; *Victorian Writer*, and *SCUM Magazine*.

www.ingramcontent.com/pod-product-compliance
Lightning Source LLC
Chambersburg PA
CBHW020326010526
44107CB00054B/2000